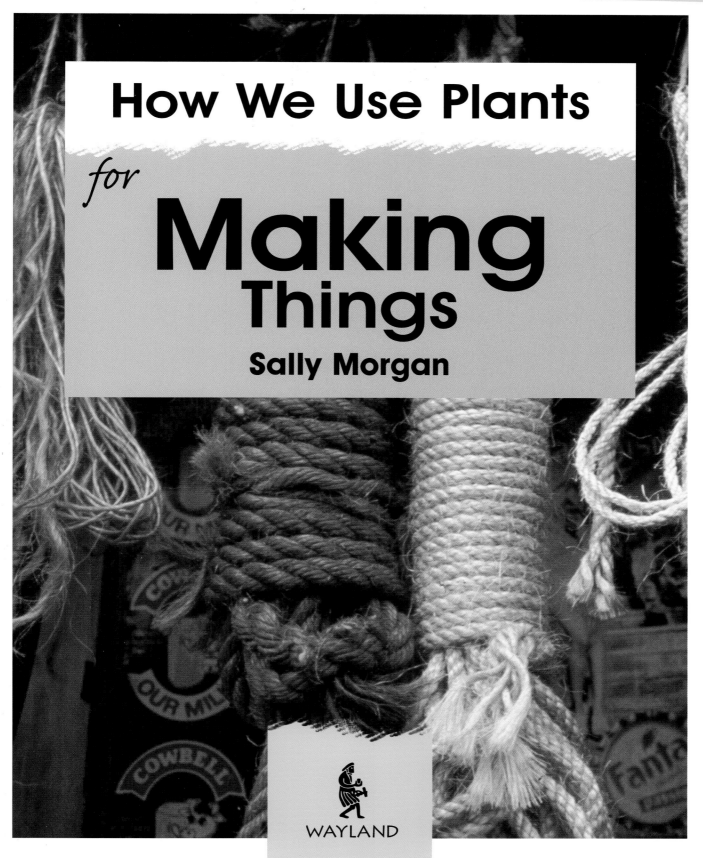

How We Use Plants

for

Making
Things

Sally Morgan

WAYLAND

First published in 2007 by Wayland

Copyright © Wayland 2007

Wayland
338 Euston Road
London NW1 3BH

Wayland Australia
Level 17/207 Kent Street
Sydney, NSW 2000

Editor: Camilla Lloyd
Designer: Matthew Lilly
Picture Researcher: Sally Morgan

Picture Acknowledgements: The author and publisher would
like to thank the following for allowing their pictures to be
reproduced in this publication: Cover: Ecoscene.
Ecoscene: 1, 4, 5, 6, 7, 8, 9, 10, 11, 12, 13, 14, 15, 16, 17,
18, 19, 20, 21, 22, 23, 24 (both), 25, 26 (all), 28.

With special thanks to Ecoscene.

British Library Cataloguing in Publication Data:
Morgan, Sally
How we use plants for making things
1. Plants, Useful - Juvenile literature
I. Title
581.6'36

ISBN: 978 07502 5062 7

Printed in China

Wayland is a division of Hachette Children's Books

Contents

Plants for making things

Plants are important because they give us food such as bread, rice, potatoes, fruits and vegetables. They also have many other uses. Look around your home and you will see many objects made from plants.

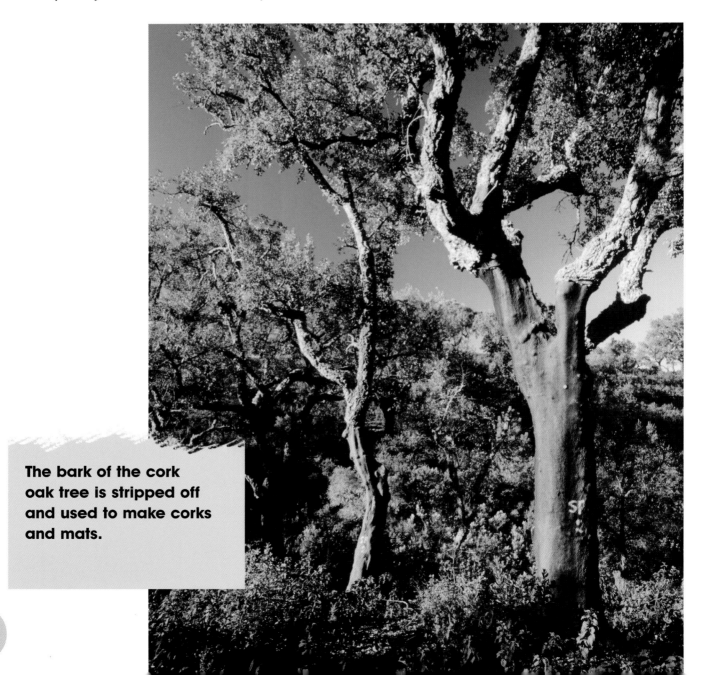

The bark of the cork oak tree is stripped off and used to make corks and mats.

4

People have used plants to make things for thousands of years. **Wood** comes from trees and is one of the world's most useful plant materials. It is used to make buildings, boats, furniture, tools and paper.

This ship is made from wood and the sails are made from canvas.

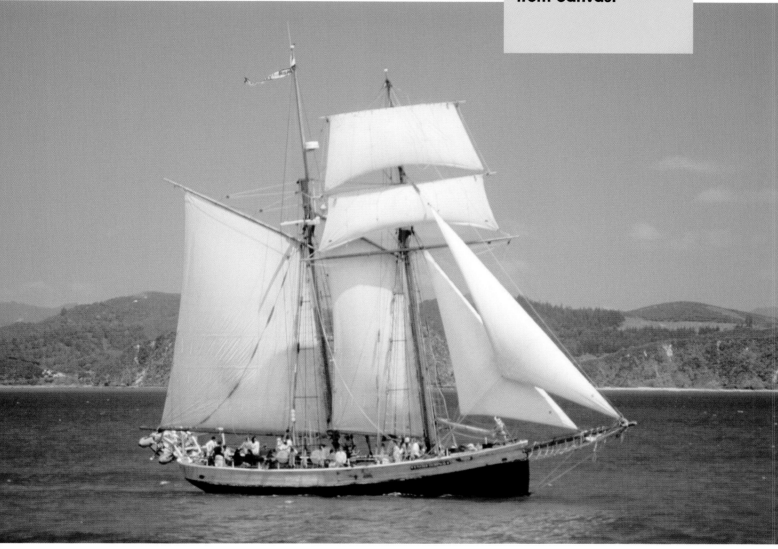

Other useful plants include the cotton plant. This produces a **fibre** that is used to make cotton **fabric**. Canvas is another useful material. It is made from the fibres of the hemp plant.

Trees for wood

Wood is an incredibly strong material. It is tough and lasts a long time. It supports the trunk of the tree and allows the tree to grow.

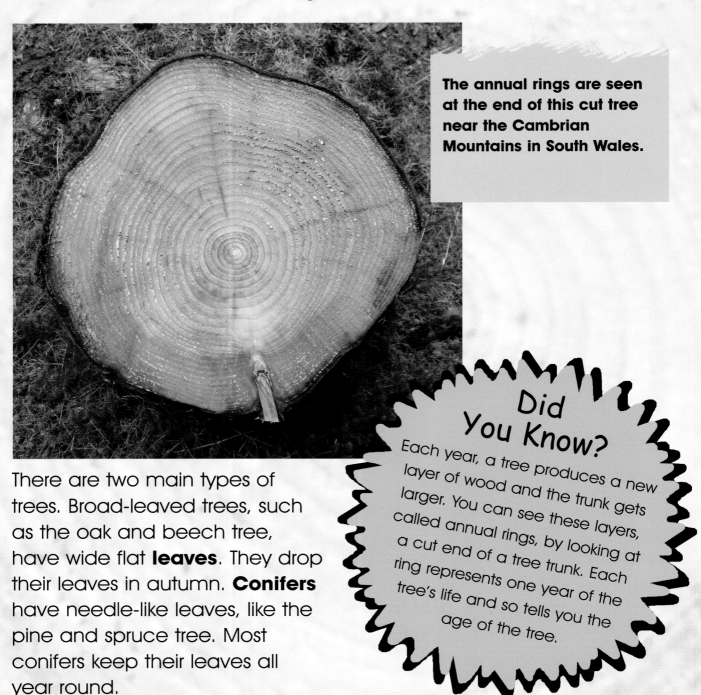

The annual rings are seen at the end of this cut tree near the Cambrian Mountains in South Wales.

There are two main types of trees. Broad-leaved trees, such as the oak and beech tree, have wide flat **leaves**. They drop their leaves in autumn. **Conifers** have needle-like leaves, like the pine and spruce tree. Most conifers keep their leaves all year round.

Did You Know?

Each year, a tree produces a new layer of wood and the trunk gets larger. You can see these layers, called annual rings, by looking at a cut end of a tree trunk. Each ring represents one year of the tree's life and so tells you the age of the tree.

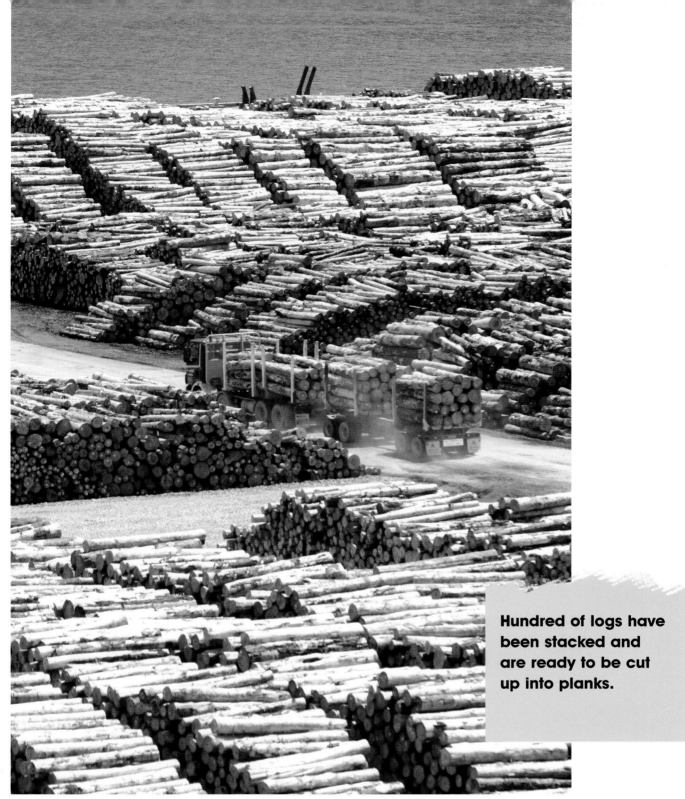

Hundred of logs have been stacked and are ready to be cut up into planks.

We collect wood by cutting down trees. Some fast-growing trees are planted as **crops** that can be **harvested** for wood after growing for about 30 or 40 years.

Making furniture

There are many types of wood used to make furniture. They differ in colour, hardness and how they look. Teak, mahogany and oak are **hardwoods** and are among the strongest woods. Conifer trees such as the pine grow faster than hardwoods but their wood is softer. They are called **softwoods**. Softwoods are not so good for making furniture because the wood is easily damaged.

Hardwoods, such as mahogany and oak, are best for carving. This carved door is in Morocco.

Did You Know?

Balsa is one of the lightest woods. It is perfect for making model boats and planes. The heaviest wood is ironwood, it can be used for outdoor furniture.

- Look around your home for doors and furniture made from wood. The most common woods that will be in your home are oak and pine. Look closely at the wood. Can you see the grain?

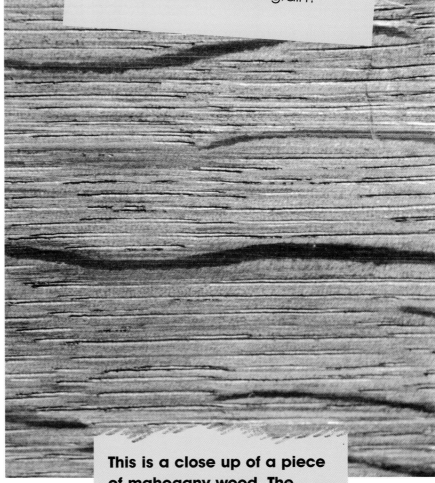

This is a close up of a piece of mahogany wood. The pattern of lines that you see is called the grain.

9

Shaping wood

Wood can be used to make all sorts of objects. It is a hard material and can be carved. The carving is done with a cutting tool that has a sharp edge like a knife. Often the carpenter draws the shape they want on the wood and then they start carving. Gradually they remove the wood until the right shape is formed. Wood for objects like furniture, doors and boats can also be **manufactured** by machines in factories.

This decorative strip of wood has been made from carved pieces of yew wood.

Did You Know?

Marquetry involves sticking small pieces of thin wood onto a surface to make a pattern. Different coloured woods are used to make an interesting picture. Jewellery boxes often have lids that have been made using marquetry.

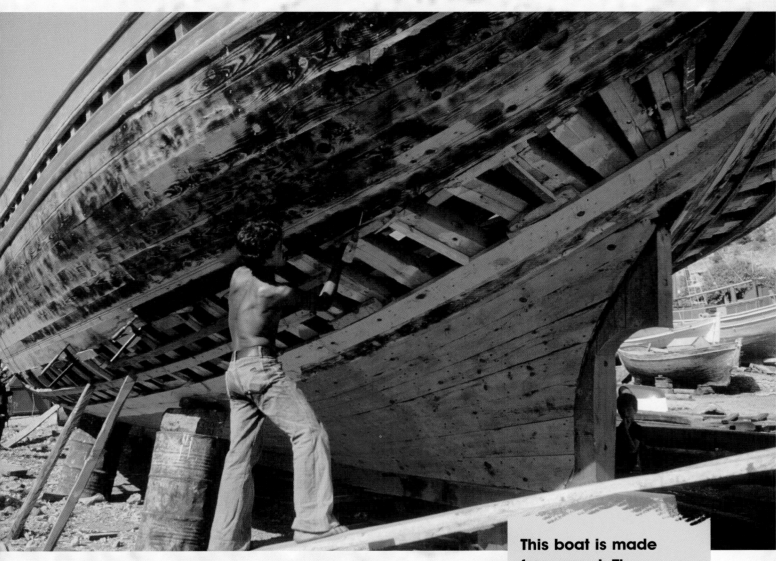

In the past, people made simple boats from logs. They carved the shape first, then hollowed out a place to sit. Wood is still a popular material for making boats.

This boat is made from wood. The carpenter shapes some of the pieces of wood by hand to make the hull (the body of the ship).

Plants for weaving

Many plants have long, flexible **stems**, which can be harvested and used for weaving. Weaving means threading the stems together to create a single object such as a basket, bag, piece of furniture or sculpture.

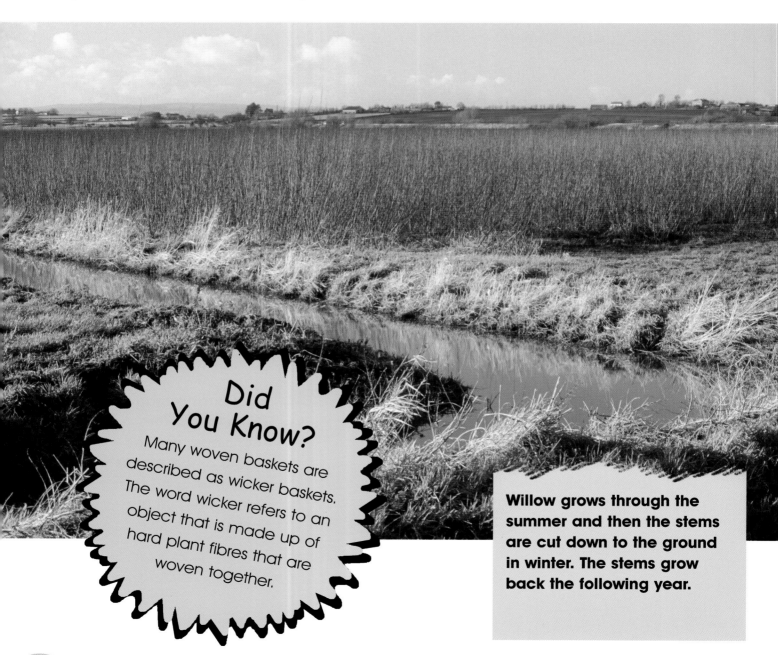

Did You Know?
Many woven baskets are described as wicker baskets. The word wicker refers to an object that is made up of hard plant fibres that are woven together.

Willow grows through the summer and then the stems are cut down to the ground in winter. The stems grow back the following year.

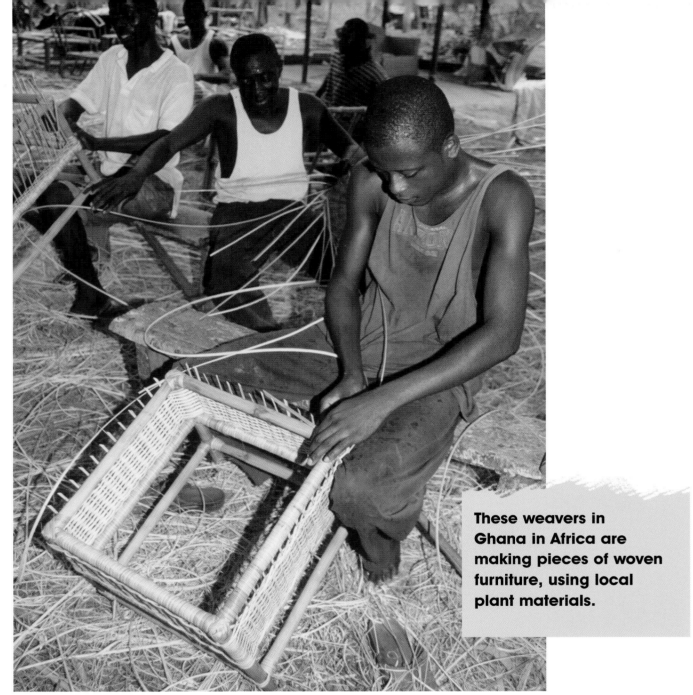

These weavers in Ghana in Africa are making pieces of woven furniture, using local plant materials.

Willow is a fast-growing plant with stems that can be harvested in the winter months. Each year new stems form. Rattans are climbing palms that grow in **tropical** rainforests. They are used to make woven furniture and mats. Other plants that can be used for weaving include grasses, rushes, reeds, hazel, bamboo and some lilies.

Making paper

Paper is made from the wood of conifers and eucalyptus trees that are grown especially to make paper. Once the trees are harvested, the logs are taken to a mill and chopped into tiny pieces. Then the pieces are mashed into a **pulp**.

Papyrus is a grass that can be used to make paper. Papyrus can grow to more than 5 metres tall. It grows near lakes and rivers.

The pulp is mixed with water and other things to form a thick paste. This is spread over a long belt where the water drains away. The pulp is flattened by rollers, dried and wound into a roll of paper.

Inside a paper mill, the pulp is spread over a belt so that the water can drain away.

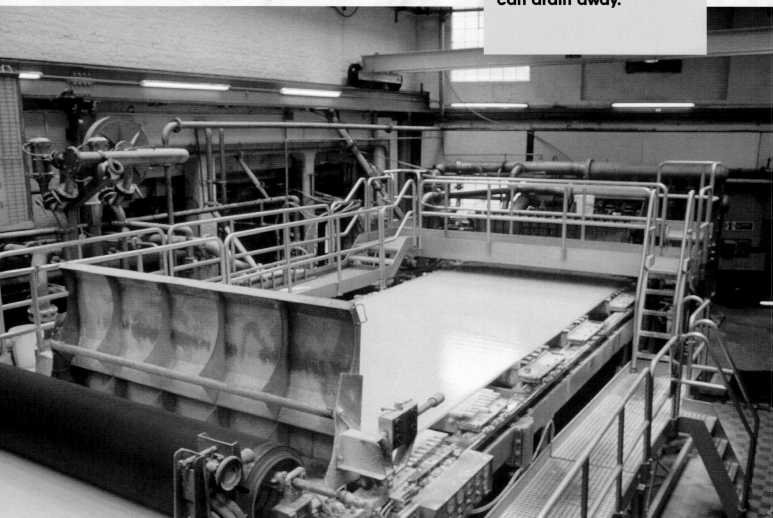

Trees are not the only plants that can make paper. Other plants such as papyrus, reeds and rushes, palms, bananas and rice can all be used to make paper.

Resin

If you make a deep cut in the bark of a pine tree, a sticky substance oozes out. This is called **resin**. Resin is used in glue, printing ink and chewing gum. It also has many other uses. It is a **raw ingredient** for paint, varnish and turpentine. Turpentine is a liquid that is used to clean paint off brushes.

Have A Go!

- When you are next walking through a pine wood or passing some conifer trees have a good look at the trunks. Can you spot any resin oozing out of the bark? Look for resin on cut stumps.

The bark of these conifer trees has been cut so that resin can be collected.

In some parts of Europe, there are large pine forests where the resin is **tapped**. The bark is cut and a small pot is placed under the cut to catch the dripping resin.

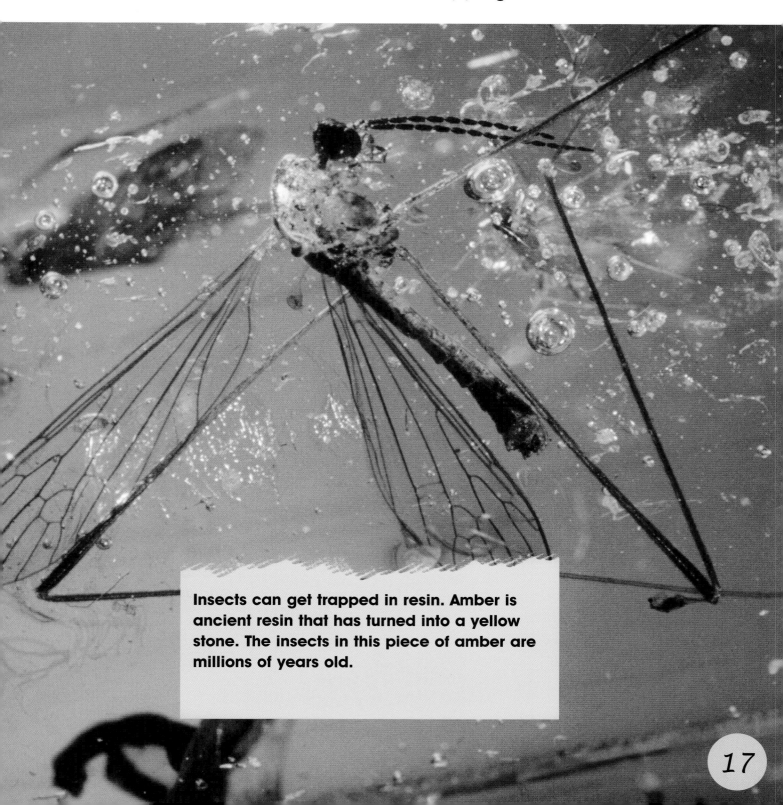

Insects can get trapped in resin. Amber is ancient resin that has turned into a yellow stone. The insects in this piece of amber are millions of years old.

Plant fibres

Have you ever tried to pull threads out of plant leaves or stems? These threads are fibres, which support and strengthen the plant. Fibres are also found in fruits and seeds.

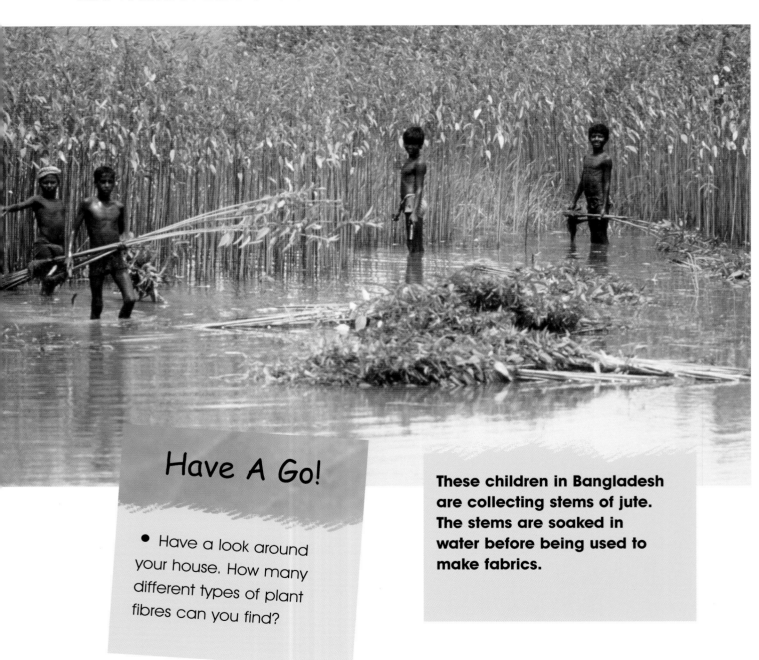

Have A Go!

- Have a look around your house. How many different types of plant fibres can you find?

These children in Bangladesh are collecting stems of jute. The stems are soaked in water before being used to make fabrics.

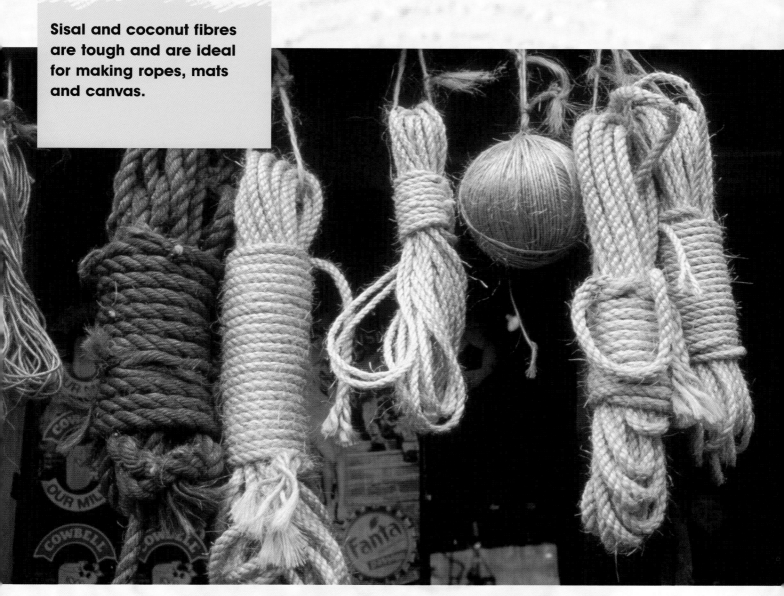

Cotton is one of the most important plant fibres but there are many other fibres. Flax is used to make linen and jute is made into hessian. Hessian is a rough fabric. Hemp is used to make canvas fabric, too. It was widely used before cotton became popular. The seed pod of the kapok tree is full of fluffy, white threads that are used as a stuffing for pillows and cushions.

Making fabrics

Plant fibres have to be harvested and cleaned. Then they are made into threads and woven into a cloth.

Workers in Turkey pick the fluffy white seedheads of the cotton by hand.

The seeds of the cotton plant are surrounded by white fibres. Long fibres are used to make cotton cloth. The seedheads are taken out and cleaned by a process called ginning. This happens in a machine called a cotton gin. The cotton fibres are put in large bags and then sent to a cotton mill where the fibres are spun into a thread. The threads are then woven into a cloth.

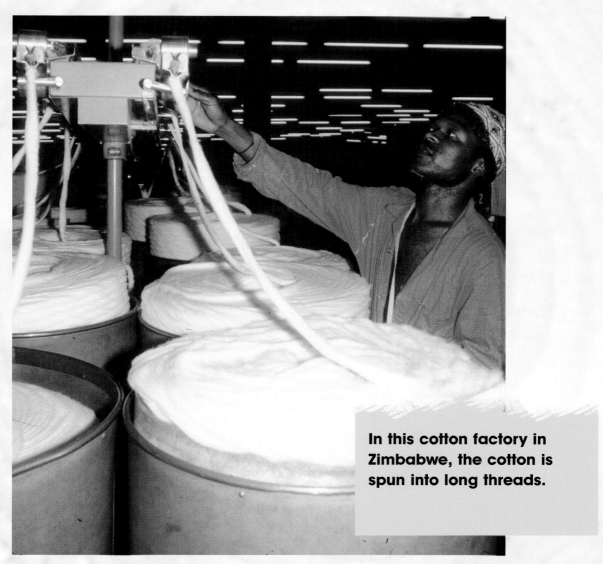

In this cotton factory in Zimbabwe, the cotton is spun into long threads.

Short, fuzzy fibres in the seedhead are called **linters**. These are used to make cotton wool, felt and soft paper.

Different fabrics

Our clothes are made from a variety of **natural** plant fibres. Cotton is one of the most common. Sometimes, cotton is mixed with a **synthetic** fibre, such as polyester, which is a fibre made from oil. Clothes made from polyester cotton are easier to look after as there are fewer creases after washing. Linen, made from flax, is used to make summer clothes as it helps people to stay cool.

The clothes on sale in this shop in England have been made from hemp.

Have A Go!

- Have a look at the washing instructions label in your clothes. The instructions depend on the fabric. Can cotton and polyester cotton be washed at the same temperature?

The sail of this African boat is made from canvas.

Fabrics made from hemp are becoming more popular. Hemp is a fibre that was used to make the denim for the original Levi jeans, until it was replaced by cotton. Hemp is a hard-wearing fabric and is used to make canvas sails as well as clothes and sandals.

Rubber

Rubber is an **elastic** material that can be stretched. When it is let go, it returns to its original shape. Rubber is used to make tyres, Wellington boots, and waterproof fabrics.

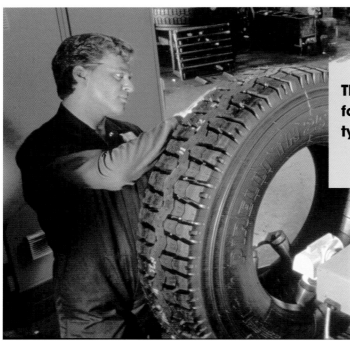

The worker in this tyre factory is checking new tyres for any faults.

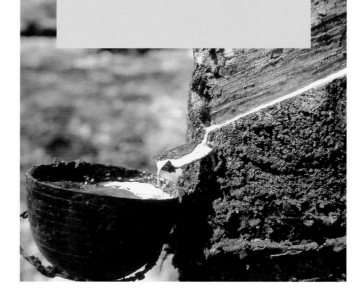

Latex oozes out of a fresh cut. The drips of latex from the bark are collected in a cup.

Rubber comes from the rubber tree, although nowadays rubber can be made **artificially**. When the bark of the tree is cut a white **latex** oozes out. The latex is collected and made into sheets. These are sent to factories to be made into many different things.

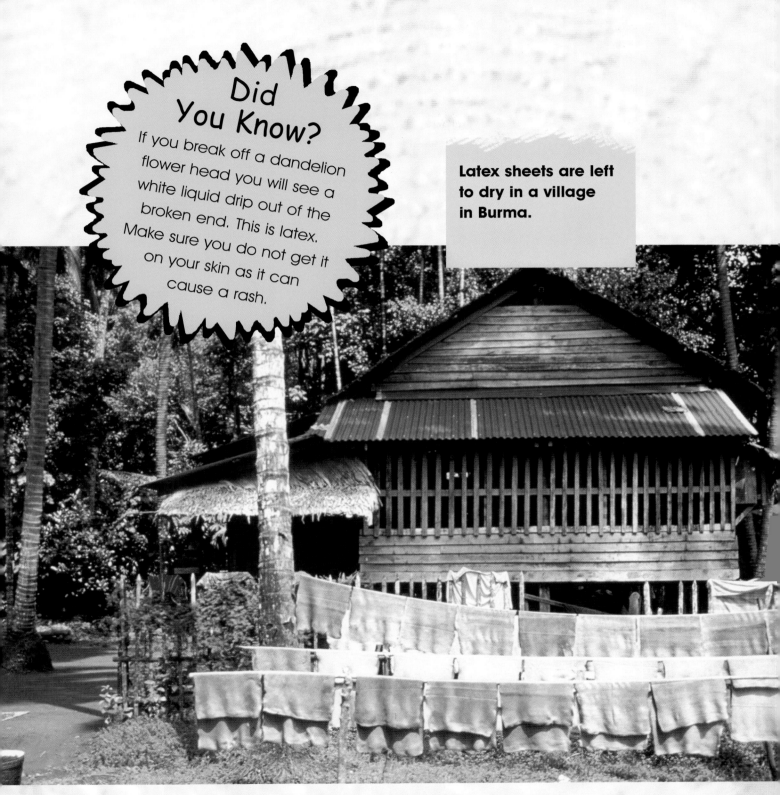

Latex sheets are left to dry in a village in Burma.

Natural rubber becomes **brittle** when it gets cold and sticky when it is hot. To stop this happening sulphur is added to the rubber at the factory. This is called **vulcanisation**.

Bamboo

Bamboo is one of the most useful plants growing in Asia. Bamboo is a type of grass. It grows in a clump, with long hollow stems and **lance-shaped leaves**. As well as being the favourite food of the giant panda, it has many other uses.

Furniture:
Bamboo can be used to make furniture and mats. It is a very popular wood in the Philippines.

Bamboo stems:
The hollow stems are of different widths. They are used in buildings and to make bridges.

Food:
Leaves and young stems are used as an animal food. We can also eat bamboo shoots and the flower seeds can be used as grain.

Cooking:
You can cook rice in bamboo pots and eat and drink from bamboo bowls and cups.

Make your own paper!

You can make recycled paper from waste paper. Ask an adult to help you. You will need about 30 sheets of used office paper, drawing pins, a wooden frame about 30 cm wide by 20 cm high (an old picture frame would be ideal), two pieces of thin wood (plyboard) larger than the frame, a piece of old net curtain, washing up bowl or tub that is large enough to take the frame, 6 kitchen cloths, a plastic bucket and glass bottles.

Step 1

Tear up the paper into tiny pieces and put in a bucket. Cover the pieces with water overnight. Using your hands squeeze and stir the soggy paper until it looks a bit like porridge.

Step 2

Pin the net to the frame with the drawing pins, making sure it is stretched tightly. The next bit is very messy so it is best to work outside. Place a piece of plyboard on the ground and cover with a kitchen cloth.

Step 3

Place the frame in the bowl and pour some pulp into it. Spread the pulp around so that it forms a thin layer over the net. Lift the frame and let the water drain away.

Step 4

Turn the frame over so that the paper is facing downwards and then place it onto the kitchen cloth. The pulp should drop off onto the kitchen cloth. Place another kitchen cloth on top of the pulp. Repeat this process to produce 5 layers of pulp.

Step 5

Place the last kitchen cloth on the top and cover with the second board. Put some heavy weights (like full bottles) on top of the board to squeeze out all the water. Leave for several hours then carefully remove the layers of paper on the kitchen cloths and leave them in a warm place to dry. When they are dry you may need to iron them on a low setting to flatten them. Ask an adult to help you.

Glossary

artificial not natural, made by people.

brittle easily broken.

conifer a type of tree with leaves that are shaped like needles.

crop a plant grown by people for a special use.

elastic stretchy. A material that can be stretched and will spring back into its original shape.

fabric cloth, material.

fibre a thread.

hardwood wood that comes from slow-growing trees.

harvested ripened crops that have been gathered from the fields.

lance-shaped leaves leaves that are longer than they are wide. They get narrower from the middle towards the tip.

latex a milky liquid produced by some plants like rubber.

leaf (pl leaves) part of a plant, a blade that is attached to the stem.

linters short, fuzzy fibres in the seedhead of a cotton plant.

manufactured to manufacture objects means to make them with machines.

marquetry designs or pictures made of thin wood.

natural from nature, the environment around us.

pulp a mush.

raw ingredient something in its natural state that is added to other things.

resin a sticky substance made by certain plants such as pine trees.

softwood wood that comes from fast-growing trees.

stem part of a plant that supports the leaves.

synthetic artificial, made by people.

tapped drained.

tropical areas of the world which lie close to the Equator and which are hot all year round.

vulcanisation when sulphur is added to rubber to stop it breaking or melting.

wood a substance made by trees that makes up much of the tree trunk.

Further information

Books

Wool and Cotton (How we Use Materials) by Rita Storey and Holly Wallace, Watts, 2006

Art from Wood by Pam Robson and Gillian Chapman, Wayland, 2005

Wood (Science Files) by Steve Parker, Heinemann Library, 2002

Wood (Resources and the Environment) by Kathryn Whyman, Watts, 2003

Websites

Arts and Crafts ideas:
http://www.artsncrafts-ideas.com/kidcraft ideas.php
Website with lots of information about ideas for arts and crafts projects.

Paper in Wisconsin:
http://www.wipapercouncil.org/fun&learning.htm

Recycle for Cornwall:
http://www.recycleforcornwall.org.uk/education/ children/activities/child-act-papier/how-to-make-paper

Creative Paperworks:
http://www.creativepaperwales.co.uk/how_ made.asp
Websites on how to make paper and papier-mâché and why recycling is important.

Answers

P18 you may be able to find four, or even more. Common ones are cotton, linen, coconut, sisal

P22 cotton can be washed at high, even boiling temperatures but polyester fibres should not be washed above 60 degrees Celsius (°C) or 140 degrees Fahrenheit (°F)

Index